Queen Kno

This Book is Dedicated

to my parents

Willie & Charlotte Crisp

Introduction

The strength of a Woman is unmatched. She is clothed with style and grace. Willing to sacrifice all that she has for what she loves.

 A Woman knows her worth regardless of what others may think of her. She is a Queen with her head held high. Rising above all the things meant to destroy her.

Appreciation

Hello Queen,

I would like to thank you for purchasing my book. The contents are meant to inspire and uplift all women. I felt the need to create a guide for us as a reminder that no matter what we have gone through there is a divine purpose for our lives. We are not our mistakes. Our experiences good or bad elevates us toward our destiny. My hope is for us all to have Self-love and to Know our Worth!

Xoxo

Queen Know your Worth

Written by:

Rashanda Crisp

Selfless

A Woman's Devotion

Written by:

Rashanda Crisp

Chapter 1

RE-INVENT

To change or make new

When you think of the word change what comes to mind? Possibly leaving a job or perhaps moving to a new home. There are many ways that we can relate to change. The most difficult change is reinventing ourselves. If you have ever gone through a traumatic experience you will not come out of it the same as you went in.

It affects us all in different ways. For example, dealing with the loss of a loved one is a very painful experience. When you have someone close to you that has been there for you whom you have lost, you never get over the pain of them being gone. You will have to make the decision to make the necessary changes in your life and find the strength to continue living without them physically.

Or maybe you have been or are currently in an abusive relationship that has caused you to lose sight of yourself. It may seem as if this is how your life is supposed to be and that there is nothing you can do to change it. The thought of leaving and starting over may cause fear of being alone. Others turn to drugs or alcohol to cover up the pain of their trauma instead of having to deal with it in a sober state of mind.

I have personally suffered the loss of loved ones and have also been in abusive relationships. I am here to tell you that the most difficult thing to change is possible. There were many times in my life when I felt that it was over, as if the pain I was experiencing was greater than the lesson I had to learn. Well, I was wrong. Pain is an emotional experience in which time heals, but if it is not dealt with and processed properly it can have a damaging long-term effect on your life. The thought of reinventing ourselves can be overwhelming but we must continue to fight. Ask yourself, are you willing to sacrifice your peace of mind and happiness for something that is causing you pain and heartache? Is it more important to be connected to the wrong person rather than being connected to your divine purpose?

The most important part of change is coming to realize that you deserve to live in peace. Being free to wake up every day with a smile, free to be yourself and to genuinely be happy. If you have invested into a relationship and it has not served you or been an advancement toward your growth as a woman, it could be that your investment is not aligned with your future.

No matter how many days we have lived, there are many more days ahead of us that we should prepare for. Why bring your past into your future when they each have their own story to tell. Do not allow your past experiences to control what is to come, instead look forward to creating new experiences. You are worthy of a good life with someone who genuinely loves you.

Once you make the decision to change your circumstances you can begin the road to acceptance.

Chapter 2

ACCEPTANCE

To acknowledge your reality

The first step of acceptance is to acknowledge your reality and admit your mistakes, we all make them. It can be exceedingly difficult to come to terms with the fact that you may have allowed yourself to be in an unhealthy or negative situation. Denial blocks your ability to focus on what is in front of you.

The process of acceptance is all about you, no one else. Begin the healing process by owning your decisions even the ones that lead you down the wrong path. The people in our lives cannot make that decision for you. We made them therefore we must accept them.

Self-accountability is the next best place to start. Be truthful with yourself when it comes to what is in your best interest.

Although we may not understand why we made certain choices, accepting our faults will relieve the burden of regret. When we go through life carrying pain from our past it remains a constant weight on our shoulders which can lead to depression. It keeps us sidetracked and hinders us from living a fulfilled life. Overcoming our past means we are a survivor.

It means you made the decision to keep pushing forward by finding the strength deep within to not give up. Be proud of having that strength and courage to endure. Never deny yourself the life you deserve.

A good place to start is by replacing negative thinking with positive thoughts. Here are just a few affirmations we can use daily to guide us in the direction of acceptance.

I am not perfect.

I have made mistakes.

I forgive myself.

I will make better choices.

I own myself the best life.

I love myself.

I am Worthy.

Change your perception of yourself, meditate in solitude. Being able to focus without any distractions allows you to put things into perspective clearer. Change your daily habits and routine.

Take all the necessary steps to change your circumstances including your environment and the company you keep that no longer serve you. Embrace how far you have come and the woman still standing. Acceptance opens the door to having the ability to unconditionally love yourself. Understand that this is a learning process which can be painful at first. Holding onto pain effects our health and our family dynamics.

There as so many choices that I made in my life that I wish I could change, but I cannot. I made the decision to not allow my past mistakes to cause me to live there. As women we do the best that we know how to do until we learn to do better.

Regret is a major factor in harboring feelings of guilt, self-blame and disappointment that can deprive us of true happiness.

Whether it is making mistakes in raising our children, having a failed relationship or not completing your own goals because of having to sacrifice for your family, regret can and will steal your joy and keep you from progressing. Never tolerate what is not beneficial to the well being of your mental and physical health. Do not compromise loving yourself for the temporary affection from someone who is not even capable of loving themselves. Embrace how far you have come and stand firm in your choices. You have overcome your worst which means your best is yet to come. Once you have achieved a new level of acceptance in your life, forgiveness will surely follow.

Chapter 3

FORGIVENESS

A conscious decision to release guilt

During the process of forgiving yourself and others is where you release any self-blame, feelings of resentment, guilt or thoughts of vengeance you may be holding on to. This does not mean forgetting, condoning or excusing anything that was harmful to you. It simply means not allowing the past to have any control over the present. As women we often tend to hold onto past situations which is very unhealthy. The decisions we may have made in our lives were perhaps not always in our best interest. Again, life is full of learning experiences that molds us into the person we were created to be. During this level of forgiveness is where you make the decision to let it all go. Leaving the past behind you is essential for your growth. Release the hurt, acknowledge the pain and use it as fuel to rid yourself of toxic selfless behavior. Develop a sense of self-worth. Formulate what you want and what is best for you. This process requires patience. Reassure yourself that you are worthy of being happy and that there are better days ahead. It is also imperative to forgive those who have wronged you or made you feel any less than what you are worth. If possible, make amends with those you love. It will be solely up to that person or people to embrace your desire to rectify the situation, you have no control over that. The one thing we do have control over is forgiving ourselves, which allows us to have control over our own mental and emotional state. Make the decision to put yourself first. By doing so does not mean that you should not care about others, it simply means that you too are a priority. Self-care is vital. Most people will appreciate those who seek forgiveness because it helps them to understand that the person who hurt them is taking responsibility for their actions. If your gesture is not embraced this means that those people have not reached a time in their own personal life where they are ready to forgive and move forward. Remember not everyone can return the love that you give so effortlessly.

Forgiveness will have a profound effect on your wellness. Now that you are on the path of forgiving yourself, take some time for self-reflection.

Colossians 3:12,13

Chapter 4

SELF-REFLECTION

Assessment of one's own character or actions

The process of self-reflection can be a hard pill to swallow. This is a time where you look at yourself from an open an honest perspective.

During my own personal self-reflection, I had to go back to when I began to live not only for myself but for my children.

As a young mother I had to grow with my children. I always did the best that I could to provide for them and to be present in their lives. Unfortunately, a lot of my choices were not always in their best interest. Managing motherhood during a time when I was still learning what life was about was truly challenging. One thing for certain is that my love for them was never unsure. I am sharing my story with you in hopes that during your moments of self-reflection no matter where you begin, you will allow yourself no matter how painful it may be to come to terms with it. Take inventory of your thoughts and feelings. Personally, I suffered through situations that could have led me down a road that I was not equipped for.

Fortunately, my destiny was greater than my mistakes. It is healthy to reflect on where you came from, what is not healthy is to live there. Life is a gift; we are given the chance each day to make better choices.

Everyone's journey has a story to tell. Some parts have a happy ending and other parts are very painful. Understand, each chapter of our lives are connected to one decision that we made on which road to take. Know that those chapters cannot be re-written.

It is okay to cry, feel regret and shame. Process all those feelings and release it. We cannot give those emotions more power than they deserve. Being human means, we all were born with free will. We were given total control over our decisions. How we deal with those choices determines the outcome of that chapter.

Closure

Finality; Letting go

Along with Self-reflection closure is another form of healing. In relationships closure is something we all would love to have when it comes down to unanswered questions or the reasoning behind the actions of others. Closure can provide acceptance of what no longer exists. Many of us have held onto anger and resentment simply because we never received a clear understanding or explanation regarding their behavior. Unfortunately, closure is something we may never receive, which is why it is important to understand that the actions of others are solely for their own accountability, it has nothing to do with anyone else. You may feel that if you would have done things differently in your relationship maybe the other person would not have treated you badly.

Or maybe if you would not have been so opinionated, the arguments would not have occurred. There is nothing you could have done to change the actions of that person. True love is unconditional and should always be reciprocated. The only closure we should seek comes from within.

Another form of closure involves family relationships.

Family; Inheritance

Most families have situations where certain members do not see eye to eye. There may be long term sibling or parent rivalry that exists for whatever reason which can divide the family. Reflect on where the rivalry began if possible, try to come up with a solution to rectify the situation if all parties are willing.

Sometimes closure and forgiveness within our own immediate family is the hardest to obtain. By the time we reach adulthood the pain and uncertainty has manifested into hostility, which makes it more difficult to restore the bond we should have between one another. Ultimately, we can not change who we are divinely connected to.

If closure is something we can not attain, let us undoubtedly continue to love one another, forgiving without judgement and knowing that the one thing in life that is not exchangeable is family.

1 Peter 4:8

Chapter 5
KNOW YOUR WORTH

Acquired sense of one's own value

Women were created with a valuable purpose in this world. We are a figure of Beauty, Love, Strength and the Nurturing ability to care for others. We would not have been created to be such profound loving beings without given the ability to love ourselves. As young girls we are often taught to be aware of our appearance.

Also to dress appropriately, speak correctly as well as acquiring proper domestic habits. While these qualities are beneficial, our internal perception of ourselves is what molds us into being a woman of substance who Knows her worth. We add value to everything we are a part of, we have made a profound contribution to society past and present.

A woman is one of the most unique beings in this world.

Although life changing events occur, some are avoidable, and some are inevitable. The decisions we make do not always produce positive outcomes, and that is okay. Not one person on this earth is without flaws. A lot of times we go through life seeking or having the expectation to be loved. Unfortunately, not everyone we encounter will be capable of giving loving with a sincere heart.

This is where discernment comes into place. You are deserving of Love, Loyalty, Honor and Respect. Our choices in relationships should not be based solely on emotion but rather by the other person's ability to love and care for you as well as possess the characteristics necessary to maintain a healthy relationship.

Relationships that are not healthy will take a toll on you. When we stay in a negative situation far beyond it's time, we begin to develop a sense of insecurity which transforms into a lack of value toward ourselves. During these times is when it is most important to re-evaluate our circumstances. The love you give should always be reciprocated. Self-worth is imperative. When you know your worth, you realize that you are deserving of someone who will cherish you and assist in maintaining that level of worth. No one can put a value on your life. No one can set the standard for you. No one can tell you that you are not worthy of being loved and treated with the utmost respect. Relying on the opinion of others diminishes your ability to see the full value of yourself. When you have requirements set in place anyone having the desire to be a part of your life must be on the same accord. You are not being selfish.

You should never allow anyone to take away your self-worth. Release any emotional baggage you may carry. Love yourself, respect yourself and demand to be treated with everything that you provide to others. Now that you understand the importance of Knowing your Worth your Self-love will shine through.

Proverbs 31:10

Chapter 6

SELF-LOVE;

Regard for one's own well-being.

As women we have so much in common. For this reason, I am sharing my story with you in hopes to inspire you to Know your Worth! Self-love is something that I struggled with for many years. I felt that because I kept myself up and lived what I thought was a "normal" life I was fulfilled.

As I got older and life continued to happen, I realized that the choices I was making, the friendships and relationships I chose offered me nothing more than to teach me that not everything that glitters is gold. I had to learn to genuinely love myself and to have discernment in who I allowed in my life. During this process I began to lose people, family and "friends" who I believed at that time were the ones who would loved me the most. People will come into your life to rob you of everything they wish they had themselves. Once you no longer serve their purpose you become too good, or I never like her anyway. Sometimes growth consists of solitude and mental recuperation. It is okay to take time out to put the pieces back together and polish your crown. Clarity reveals all truths.

Self-Love is not an option; it is a necessity. Self-care should also be a daily requirement set in place to sustain your mental and physical stability. Women are responsible for caring for the children, being a partner to a spouse, maintaining the home all while working a job. Some of us also attend school to further our careers. Although we wear many hats, we cannot neglect our own needs.

During the process of self-care is where we allow ourselves to recharge, while rediscovering the power within ourselves. Create short-term goals which can help to build confidence and a sense of accomplishment.

As women we tend to be our own biggest critic. Instead of focusing on our own unique qualities, we often deprive ourselves of self-regard.

When we acknowledge the fact that we too require care

and support our perception of ourselves strengthens. As women we naturally protect what is most significant in our lives often excluding ourselves.

In life we learn to adapt to our surroundings. We become emotionally involved in what we choose to invest our time and energy into, which often takes away from our own personal needs. The relationships we encounter throughout life tend to pile up into emotional baggage when we do not allow ourselves time to heal in between and release any negativity we may carry. Whether good or bad each relationship leaves a lasting impression on our lives, in turn we become what we allow. How we love ourselves should not be based on the ability of someone else being able to love you. Self-Love requires boundaries to be set for yourself.

Implement limitations on what you except in your life. One way to protect yourself is to listen your intuition. Whether you are involved in a friendship or personal relationship you should always take inventory, meaning evaluate the relationships. If it does not add to your personal growth and to the quality of your life, it can be a hinderance.

Surround yourself with strong minded, positive people who will be a beneficial, positive impact in your life. A support system is a great place to start.

MY SISTER'S KEEPER

Women supporting and uplifting one another

As women we have an obligation to be supportive of one another. Often women look at one another and instantly begin to criticize or speak negatively about them. Their opinion of them is instant without even knowing what struggles they may be dealing with. This type of behavior is toxic, not only toward the other woman but towards our self as well. Before we start to judge others, we should examine how we view ourselves. Imagine the pain of how difficult it is to be heartbroken or to feel like your all alone. People who are internally broken usually cannot see the importance of supporting someone else. They may feel that the people in their lives have been a disappointment to them, and that they never had anyone to rely on. So, in retrospect how can you give to someone what you feel you have never received. I can relate to being that someone who felt alone or feeling that no one would ever understand what I have been through. As I have matured, I have made the decision to forgive myself and work toward releasing all the emotional baggage I was carrying. Though this process takes time and patience I am inspired to help other women who are experiencing similar situations.

As women we have so much more in common that we would like to admit. Through authors, movies and social platforms there are so many of us today who have made the decision to speak out on relationships, abuse and many other situations that have affected our lives in a heartfelt way. It takes courage to allow yourself to be heard, this can be an exceedingly difficult decision to make. Fear of being judged and looked upon as someone who is damaged can be extremely challenging. Which is why it is so important to be free of guilt toward ourselves. Your story is not yours alone, so many of us have experienced the same situations in life just in different forms. Which is why it is imperative to allow yourself to acknowledge the hurt and past mistakes to begin the process of healing. Sharing your story can be an inspiration to others. Having empathy towards our sisters can make a world of difference. Let us explore together ways of becoming our sister's keeper:

We can start by being non-judgmental toward one another which shows that your intentions are true and that her well- being is most important. Uplift her with encouraging words, take time to share your experiences which shows emotional support.

Being a good listener shows that her feelings are valid and deserves to be addressed. You can be of much needed support by being available more often. If you are unable to respond to a text or phone call immediately, always respond when you have the time.

Have a girl's night out. Allow time to relax and not think about the things that weigh you down. Focus on the moment and appreciate the things that you are grateful for. Express your desire to see her happy.

There are so many ways that we can be of support to our fellow sisters. Keep in mind that we all have the same trials and lessons in this life. Together in unity we stand stronger. Building bonds with one another by making ourselves accessible to those who may need a shoulder to lean on.

Be that someone who is there for others when they are not able to be there for themselves. We all need a support system, a trusted circle of friends which can help us to realize that we are not alone. If you feel like you have no one to reach out to, there are women's support groups available within your community. Please feel free to reach out to myself if needed through my email listed at the end of this guide.

As women we should always be our Sister's Keeper.

Proverbs 27:17

Epilogue

The worth of a Woman is priceless. Her value far outweighs her appearance. It is difficult to figure out her most inner thoughts without understanding where she has been. The road she travels is never an easy one. She carries herself as if nothing can reach her. All while suppressing what truly is hurting her. She is a force to be reckoned with. Once she realizes her worth there is no one or nothing that can stop her. Crown up Queens and show the world that you are destined for greatness.

My Story,

I was born and raised in Southern California; The last daughter born of five girls. I was blessed to be raised by both my parents. My father was a machinist, and my mother was in the medical field as well other occupations. My solid foundation growing up allowed me to enjoy my childhood. My parents remained married for over 30 years despite separation during my teenage years. I always knew that no matter what we went through as a family we would always remain close. I attended all my school years In Los Angeles. In my teenage years I became a mother to my first child my daughter, after having her my life was forever changed. I had to grow up and make adult decisions at an early age due to my choices.

I held multiple jobs in administration and customer service to provide for my family. I did not always make the best choices in relationships. I was disappointed in myself for not loving myself more. Ultimately, I accepted my past struggles and became grateful for those hard lessons that molded me into the strong independent woman that I am today.

In 2016 while grieving the loss of my Mother I began designing women's apparel while in search of my purpose and to honor her and everything she taught me. In 2017 my clothing line "Gracious Tees" was established, a brand of Women's fashion apparel inspiring Self-love and Knowledge of Self-worth. Two years later I was inspired to write my first book entitled "Queen Know your Worth". Which was followed by my second book entitled "Selfless" A Woman's Devotion.

My desire for us all as women is to find strength in our journey. When we know our worth, we can never be undervalued. Adjust your crown and always walk with your head held high.

xoxo

Author's Contact Information

Business Email:

Gracioustees@gmail.com

Facebook Women's Support Group:

Women of Grace

National Domestic Violence Hotline:

1-800-799-7233

Apparel Website:

Gracioustees.com

Made in the USA
Middletown, DE
22 July 2022